Tools We Use
EMTs

Dana Meachen Rau

Marshall Cavendish
Benchmark
New York

Emergency! Someone is hurt.

They need help right away.

Emergency Medical Technicians (EMTs) come to help.

The EMT drives an *ambulance*.

The EMT turns on the *siren*.

She turns on lights that flash.

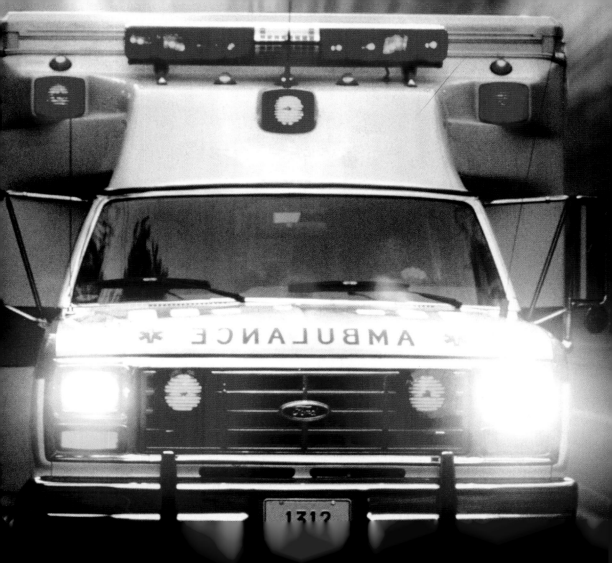

The siren and lights tell cars to move away.

The ambulance needs to get there fast.

An ambulance carries everything the EMT needs.

It is like a hospital room.

EMTs use stretchers to move people in and out.

A stretcher is like a rolling bed.

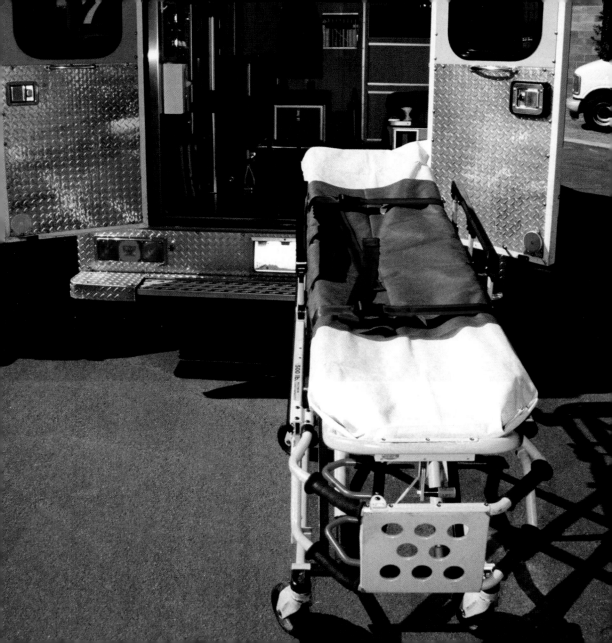

Sometimes EMTs wear masks and rubber gloves.

They do not want to spread germs.

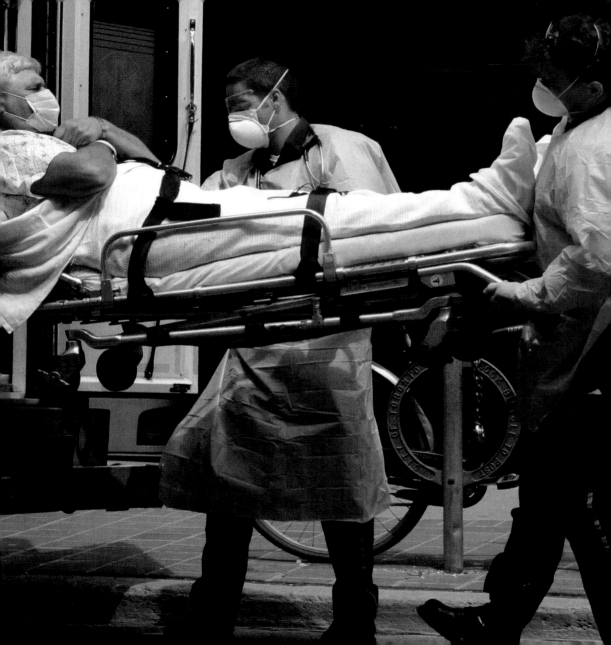

EMTs carry a drug box.

This box is filled with medicine.

Sometimes a sick person's heart stops beating.

A machine can make it beat again.

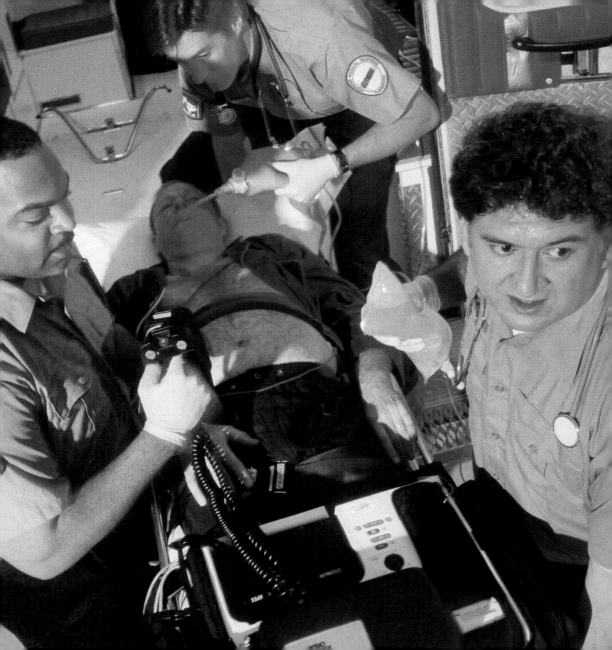

A tank holds *oxygen*.

A sick person breathes the oxygen through a mask.

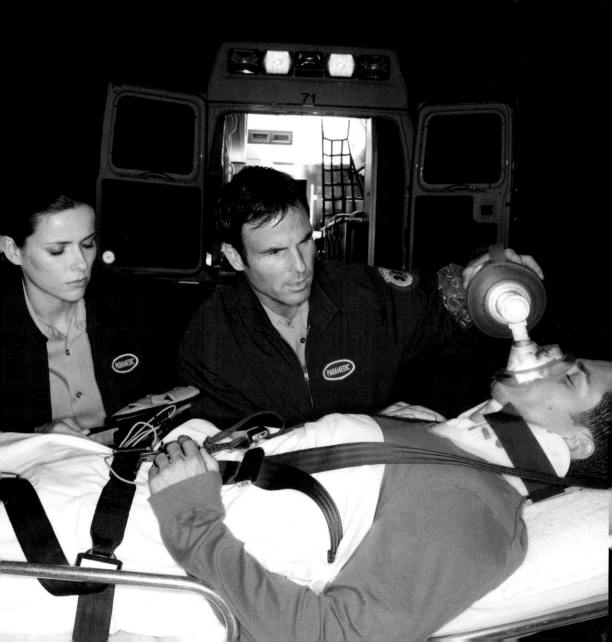

EMTs cover cuts with large *bandages*.

They use lots of small bandages, too.

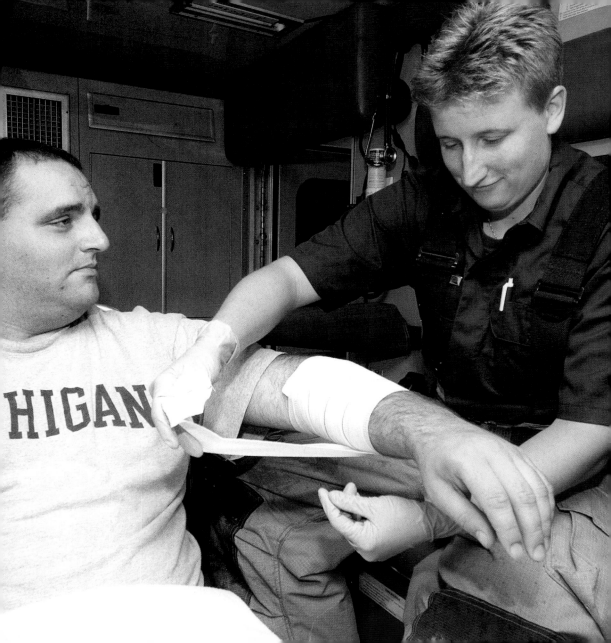

EMTs talk to the hospital on a radio.

They tell the hospital they are coming.

EMTs work hard to help people.

The tools they use save lives.

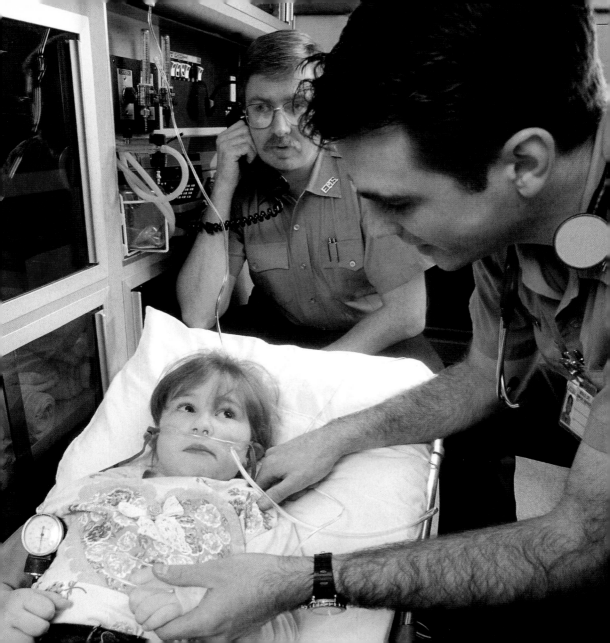

Tools EMTs Use

ambulance

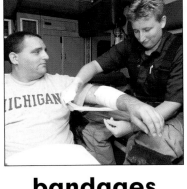

bandages

drug box

masks

oxygen

radio

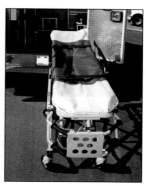

stretcher

Challenge Words

ambulance (AM-byoo-luhns) A special truck that carries people to the hospital.

bandages (BAN-dij-es) Pieces of cloth and sticky plastic tape that cover a cut.

oxygen (OX-i-juhn) A gas that helps sick people breathe.

siren (SIGH-ruhn) A loud noise from an ambulance to tell cars to move out of the way.

29

Index

Page numbers in **boldface** are illustrations.

About the Author

Dana Meachen Rau is an author, editor, and illustrator. A graduate of Trinity College in Hartford, Connecticut, she has written more than one hundred fifty books for children, including nonfiction, biographies, early readers, and historical fiction. She lives with her family in Burlington, Connecticut.

The author would like to thank Lisa Shelanskas, volunteer paramedic for Suffield Ambulance, for her help with this book.

With thanks to the Reading Consultants:

Nanci Vargus, Ed.D., is an Assistant Professor of Elementary Education at the University of Indianapolis.

Beth Walker Gambro received her M.S. Ed. Reading from the University of St. Francis, Joliet, Illinois.

Marshall Cavendish Benchmark
99 White Plains Road
Tarrytown, New York 10591-9001
www.marshallcavendish.us

Text copyright © 2008 by Marshall Cavendish Corporation

Library of Congress Cataloging-in-Publication Data

Rau, Dana Meachen, 1971–
EMTs / by Dana Meachen Rau.
p. cm. — (Bookworms. Tools we use)
Summary: "Introduces the tools EMTs use in their work"—Provided by publisher.
Includes index.
ISBN 978-0-7614-2660-8
1. Emergency medicine—Equipment and supplies—Juvenile literature.
2. Emergency medical services—Equipment and supplies—Juvenile literature. I. Title. II. Series.
RC86.5.R38 2007
616.02'5—dc22
2006035146

Editor: Christina Gardeski
Publisher: Michelle Bisson
Designer: Virginia Pope
Art Director: Anahid Hamparian

Photo Research by Anne Burns Images

Cover Photo by *Jay Mallin Photos*

The photographs in this book are used with permission and through the courtesy of:
SuperStock: pp. 1, 25, 29C Lisette Le Bon; pp. 9, 11, 19 age fotostock.
Corbis: pp. 3, 7, 28TL Gabe Palmer; pp. 15, 28BR Reuters; pp. 21, 29L Royalty Free.
Jay Mallin Photos: pp. 5, 17, 23, 28TR, 28BL.
Jupiter Images: pp. 13, 29R Brand X/Morey Milbradt; p. 27 Corbis.

Printed in Malaysia
1 3 5 6 4 2